STILL STANDING

KATHARINE QUARMBY

Badger
LEARNING

Badger Publishing Limited
Oldmedow Road,
Hardwick Industrial Estate,
King's Lynn PE30 4JJ

Telephone: 01553 816 082

www.badgerlearning.co.uk

2 4 6 8 10 9 7 5 3 1

Still Standing

ISBN 978-1-78837-829-1

Commissioning Editor: Sarah Rudd
Copyeditor: Rachel Rowland
Designer: Adam Wilmott

This book contains references to bullying.

Thank you to Gabriel, Hannah, and the staff and students from Stoke Newington School for sharing their advice, knowledge and experiences.

I am also hugely grateful to Beth Morrison, Deirdre Shakespeare, and others in organisations that challenge the inappropriate use of restraint and seclusion in schools.

CHAPTER ONE

Mr Harrington thought he knew it all.

Worse than that, he wanted our form to be his experiment in discipline and rewards. Although he was new, he already had a reputation. I'd heard he broke the record for the most detentions given in a single week. He was never going to be anyone's favourite teacher. It was only a matter of time before I got in serious trouble with him, being how I am.

I can concentrate no problem, but I can't sit still easily. It's not my fault. My leg jiggles at a hundred miles an hour when I sit in class, and that's on a good day. It's my way of focussing. It's not a bad thing, and it's not as if I'm allowed to wear headphones at school, so this has to do.

Mum and Dad have taken me to the doctor a few times to get extra support, but apparently, I don't need it. My parents haven't given up. They keep trying.

The first time I saw Mr Harrington, we clashed. I sat down, minding my own business, zipping and unzipping my pencil case. Every time I opened it, I counted the number of pens and pencils inside — quietly though, under my breath, not disturbing anyone.

"NOT in my class, thank you very much," he said. He snatched the pencil case off my desk.

"But, sir—"

"No buts," Mr Harrington interrupted. "This classroom will be silent unless I say otherwise."

My mouth fell open as I watched him slam it down on his desk, not caring about the expensive drawing pencils inside. Mum would be furious if they were broken. We go to a specialist art shop to buy them, and she jokes she could have a weekend at a spa for the prices they charge.

Someone sniggered at the back of the room. Mr Harrington scowled, and the class immediately fell silent.

He was a hundred per cent the worst teacher but should have been my favourite. He was my maths teacher too, and maths is my best class. That lesson should have allowed me to show him I was smart. That there was more to me than my jiggling leg. But after our first meeting, I knew immediately that being in Mr Harrington's maths class would only double my chances of getting in trouble.

CHAPTER TWO

The main problem was Mr Harrington wanted to be popular with the students. He liked to give out prizes and merit points to whoever he thought deserved them.

That afternoon in maths, I sat down and desperately tried to control my body so that he couldn't pick on me.

It didn't help.

"I'm giving out a prize to the person who can sit next to Avery," Mr Harrington said with a chuckle. "I know I couldn't."

The whole class fell silent.

I stared down at the polished floor and imagined a giant void opening up and sucking me through it, swallowing me whole, taking me away from the gawking faces and removing me from the most embarrassing moment of my entire life.

Was I so awful that people couldn't bear to sit beside me? I blinked back tears, and it took the most tremendous effort not to jiggle my leg. I did not want any more comments today. I didn't take in a word of the lesson and only pretended to write down today's equations in my workbook.

At the end of the class, I threw everything into my bag and swung it onto my back, even though I usually needed to complete the ritual of sorting everything into the correct compartments before I zipped it up. I sprinted out of the room as fast as I could. I needed to be on my own.

I escaped to a part of the playground where nobody went — the gardening area.

Wafts of mint and rosemary enveloped me as I sat on one of the raised beds to eat lunch. Mum had candles that smelled similar at home, so I found the gardening area relaxing, and I was nearly one hundred per cent sure no one would bother me here.

I ate the same thing every day: carrots, hummus, flatbreads, a satsuma and salt and vinegar crisps. They were neatly separated in my lunch box, just as I liked it. Eating everything in order usually calms me, but it wasn't working. Mr Harrington had messed up my routines.

I felt my cheeks burn. I remembered Mr Harrington smirking at me. He was trying to be funny, but I wasn't some joke to use to gain points with the class.

Suddenly, a flash of orange caught my eye. A fox! It looked curious, nose to the ground but eyes observing me. It looked painfully thin, its ribs jutting out at harsh angles.

I placed four carrot batons on the ground and didn't make a sound. It came closer, clearly desperate for something to eat. It was almost within touching distance.

"OI!"

I jumped out of my skin, and the fox dashed off in fright, its little legs skidding as it scrabbled to get away. In a flash, it disappeared through a hole in the fence. I wished I could do the same.

My stomach twisted. I'd know that voice anywhere. Mr Harrington.

CHAPTER THREE

"We have a ZERO tolerance policy for feeding animals in this school," Mr Harrington shouted as he marched towards me.

Why, out of everywhere in this entire school, was Mr Harrington in this hidden corner of the playground?

"Zero tolerance," he repeated. He stood directly in front of me. "That's another behaviour point for you."

I tried to find the words, any words, to get this teacher out of my space, but they wouldn't come. I jumped up, snapping my lunch box shut and shoving it into my backpack, and fled to the toilets.

I sat in a cubicle until it was time for afternoon registration. I knew, I just knew, that Mr Harrington would mention it. He seemed to delight in embarrassing me in front of the class, so why would he miss this opportunity? Some people didn't care when teachers called them out, but I did. I liked to keep a low profile. It suited me.

I walked into class with my eyes on the ground and sat down as quickly as possible, breathing a sigh of relief when I realised Mr Harrington wasn't there yet.

"Where were you at lunch?" asked my best friend, Mia. "I was looking for you everywhere."

I was about to explain, but then Mr Harrington rushed in, out of breath.

"I've got a class notice for you all. I've been to see the head of year about an incident in the gardening area."

He looked over the class, his eyes snagging on me for a beat longer than the rest.

"I found a pupil there feeding a wild animal. This is strictly forbidden. A fed fox is a dead fox, and feeding it puts its life in danger. The next time it happens, the pupil will be excluded. You have been warned."

Whispers broke out around me.

"Whoever did that is an idiot."

"Poor fox. How could someone be so stupid?"

I shrank down in my chair in shame. He hadn't mentioned my name, at least.

But at the end of the lesson, Mr Harrington bellowed, "Avery, I want a word with you."

My breathing became sharp and shallow. The rest of the class piled out, throwing glances my way. Now, they all knew it was me who had fed the fox. They were going to hate me.

I saw Mia hovering at the door as Mr Harrington closed it, a worried look on her face. She would end up being late for next period if she waited.

I tried to listen to Mr Harrington as he repeated everything he'd said, as if I hadn't heard him the first time. I nodded frantically, wanting him to hurry up so me and Mia could get to lesson.

The bell went, and I struggled to keep still. I was desperate to escape. I hated being late, but I hated the idea of Mia getting in trouble because of me even more.

Mia was the best friend I could ask for. We've been friends for ages. She's really quiet, and neat and tidy as well. She didn't mind if we just sat together and chilled. Sometimes, I'd put on my headphones, she'd put in her wireless earpods, and we'd listen to the same music.

"You're not even listening, are you, Avery?" Mr Harrington asked with a sigh.

"Yes, sir. I am, sir. But I need to get to my next—"

"Go on then, get out," he said, interrupting me. He turned his back.

I rushed out, grabbing Mia's hand as I flew through the door. We ran down the empty corridors, keeping an eye out for staff who would yell at us for running. The school motto flashed by, painted extra large across one of the walls. *Strive for excellence. Lead with Kindness*. Great motto, right? Clearly, it only applies to students, not teachers.

We darted into our next class, the teacher raising her eyebrows at us but thankfully not saying anything.

I couldn't concentrate that lesson. Mia kept asking if I was OK, but I knew I'd get upset if I tried to speak about the fox.

I was feeling embarrassed enough without being labelled emotional too. Best to keep my head down, stay inside my comfort zone.

I was relieved when school finished. I could go home and relax. But that sense of ease that would wash over me when I walked through my front door didn't happen.

The evening passed in a blur. After dinner, it was my turn to unload the dishwasher. I put the tableware neatly in the cupboards, all the same distance apart. I couldn't get it right, no matter how often I lined them up. I growled in frustration.

"You alright there, Avery?" Dad asked.

I just nodded and took myself off to my room. I sat at my desk and lined my coloured paints up in colour-gradient order. Usually, if I painted for ten or fifteen minutes, my mind settled enough to go to bed. Not tonight. I knew I wouldn't sleep, and I was right.

CHAPTER FOUR

It was a cupboard once. They were going to lock me in a cupboard. They call it the seclusion room, but it's a glorified cell. It's so tiny you could only fit two people inside, and there were no windows.

Time out, they called it. The behaviour mentor gripped my arm, and it was starting to hurt. She flicked on a light, stood back, and tried to usher me in.

"Avery, please, don't make this worse for yourself. You're on the edge of being suspended. Just a quick time out, and you're free to go," she said. She waved her arm, encouraging me to enter the gloomy space.

I HATED small spaces. I had an actual fear of them. But the behaviour mentor was not going to give up. I took a deep breath and stepped inside.

She looked at my face. "Listen, Avery, I'll be right outside, OK?" she said gently.

The door slammed behind me. At least she hadn't locked it.

The harsh white light from the bare lightbulb was hurting my eyes. The room was utterly bare, so there was nothing to count to try and keep calm. The chemical smell of fresh paint mixed with musty, damp wood made me feel sick.

I closed my eyes and leaned my head against the wall. I only realised I was crying when I felt the tears track down my cheeks. I tried to control my breathing just like Dad taught me. In and out, in and out. Count up to four, and hold your breath at the top. Down for four, hold your breath at the bottom.

A burst of laughter from outside the room interrupted my counting. I heard two people chatting, completely unaware that I was losing my shit in here.

I tried to slow my breathing again, but the sobs shaking my body kept breaking the pattern. How could anyone do this to me? I felt like a criminal.

I slid down the wall, curling up into a ball. I hit the floor, wishing my mum or dad would come and save me.

I didn't deserve this. All I'd done was stick up for my friend.

***

It had started in maths. Mr Harrington was always stressed when it was a single period. He said it's better to have doubles for maths so he can explain things properly.

He rushed through the homework quickly, but it was easy for me, so I didn't bother to write down his explanations.

I was drawing on my planner when he spotted me.

"Avery, you need to listen up," he demanded. "Stop mucking around drawing cartoons. I'm disappointed in you."

I heard some people laugh at me, and I closed my eyes, wishing I would disappear.

Then, it was afternoon registration. Mr Harrington again. I couldn't avoid him. He was everywhere.

"Prize-giving time, everyone!" he shouted at the class with a smile. "And I want to give out a special prize today."

Everyone sat up a bit taller, hoping they'd done something to deserve one of Mr Harrington's special prizes.

They were given out for good deeds and were just as legendary as his detentions. The last one he gave out was a £100 gaming voucher.

"The winner of the special prize is... Mia!"

Mia looked up in amazement.

"Oh, thanks, sir. What have I done to win this?"

"I've awarded you a prize..." he said, pausing for effect, "for sitting next to Avery."

I was stunned. Had I heard that right? I looked at Mia, mortified that she might sit beside me because it was seen as a good deed.

But Mia was frowning. "I don't want it," she said flatly. "Avery's my friend. I like sitting next to her."

Mr Harrington blinked in surprise. "Are you sure?"

"Yes, I'm sure," Mia snapped at him.

My mouth opened in shock. She always said "sir" and "miss" and made an effort to be polite to the teachers. I hadn't even heard her be rude to her mum, and now she was giving Mr Harrington a death stare.

"Oh, erm..." Mr Harrington stuttered. He awkwardly shuffled papers on his desk. "No prize-giving today, then. Off you all go."

But before anyone moved, words tumbled out of me.

"Please, sir, Mia should get the prize. She's got top marks for maths this week AND cleared the school herb garden. She should get a prize for that."

Mr Harrington ignored me and continued to tidy his desk. I clenched my fists and tried to stay calm, but it was bang out of order.

The class watched, their eyes going back and forth between Mr Harrington and me.

I stood up. "Please, sir, this isn't fair on Mia."

Maybe I shouted that bit because it wasn't Mia's fault. She always stood up for me and was a good friend. She shouldn't be punished for that.

Mr Harrington shouted back, and then I did lose my cool because he had.

CHAPTER FIVE

At last, the door to the cupboard opened. I scrambled to my feet and stumbled out, gulping in the fresh air.

How long had I been in there? It felt like hours.

"You need to go to the head of year's office," the behaviour mentor said. "Your mum is waiting there."

Mum! I ran all the way, lungs bursting, but I was desperate to be held by someone who cared about me, understood me. Typically, hugs weren't my thing, but right then, I couldn't think of anything I needed more.

Mum was sitting with her back to the door when I went in. She jumped up and wrapped me in her arms.

The head of year, Mrs Singh, looked stern. Mr Harrington sat next to her. I'm not great at reading people's faces — but I thought he looked a bit nervous.

The head of year cleared her throat. She did that a lot when she had things to say.

"I heard from Mr Harrington that Avery was disruptive today in class."

A silence. I didn't know what to say or where to start. Disruptive? I felt like Mr Harrington had been disrupting my life since he started at this school!

"Avery, what do you have to say for yourself?" Mrs Singh asked.

I couldn't speak. I just couldn't. I breathed in, up to four, and paused.

Back down the ladder till I breathed out. My mind cleared a bit. Mum was here. I was safe.

I managed to choke out a summary, missing out the prize-giving part as it was just too embarrassing for me to relive.

After an awkward pause, Mum asked, "So, you put her in seclusion?" Her voice was sharp as needles.

She knew how that would have felt for me. I can't even be in a room without an open window. Our house is cold all the time, but it makes me feel safe and calm.

"Obviously, nobody wants to send a young person to seclusion, Mrs Sinclair," Mr Harrington barked. "But Avery was acting out, and I had no choice."

"It's Ms Sinclair" Mum snapped.

"And I'd thank you not to say my daughter was acting out. She may have been reacting to something in her environment that she found challenging. What happened right before Avery started shouting?"

"I gave her neighbour a prize for sitting next to her and not being disturbed by her constant jiggling leg."

I put my head in my hands to hide my humiliation. When the room stayed deadly silent, I dared to peek out.

Mrs Singh looked horrified, and my mum's face was white, as if all the blood had drained away.

Mum spoke through gritted teeth, pausing between every word.

"You put my daughter in seclusion because she was upset AFTER you shamed her in front of her whole class?"

Oh no. Mum's face flushed bright red, right up to the tips of her ears. I knew what that meant. She was angry. Furious. Absolutely seething.

Mr Harrington shifted uncomfortably. Mum gave him her best death stare.

I thought I'd better pipe up before Mum lost it.

"It wasn't fair on Mia. She deserved the prize for being kind. I was only trying to tell Mr Harrington how I felt. I wanted to stick up for my friend."

Mum grabbed my hand and squeezed it.

Mrs Singh finally spoke. "This is very serious," she said, staring straight at Mr Harrington. "Very serious indeed. We will be looking into this incident. We will not have pupil-shaming in this school."

Mr Harrington looked down at the floor. I wondered if he hoped for a giant void to open and swallow him whole.

"I am disappointed, Mr Harrington," Mum said sternly. "You can expect to hear from us formally."

Then Mum pulled me up, our hands still linked, and we marched out of the office without a goodbye.

CHAPTER SIX

I couldn't help but smile as I watched the caretaker hammer new shelves into the wall. The seclusion room was being transformed back into a printer cupboard, and you wouldn't find one person in the school who was unhappy about it.

The thing is, I discovered that our school wasn't even the worst culprit. There were schools where kids were zipped up in weird tents for behaviour 'issues'. Mum and Dad had written in their letter: *Why not try to understand what's going on instead?* And it worked.

"Your mum and dad are amazing," raved Mia.

"Who would have thought our whole school behaviour policy would change because of one fierce email written by Ms Sinclair!"

"You've never read my mum's writing," I laughed. "She's so good with her words she could sell sand at the beach."

"Maybe she can do something about the school dinners next?" Mia joked back.

"Way beyond even her superpowers," I said with raised eyebrows.

It felt good to be laughing about the situation now. It certainly didn't feel funny at the time.

In the end, it worked out well. The first thing to happen was a school assembly on neurodiversity and supporting young people with disabilities. People who always thought of me as the weird kid now understood me better and made an effort with me.

I don't know what happened behind the scenes with Mr Harrington, but he seemed different.

"I'm so sorry, Avery," he said in our meeting. "I need to understand neurodiversity more. It didn't get taught during training. I thought I was supposed to be strict."

It's amazing what you can change by standing up for what you believe is right. For the first time in weeks, my mind felt clear.

The caretaker left, and I breathed in the smell of fresh wood. I reached into the printer cupboard and flicked off the light, happily closing the door behind me.

AUTHOR NOTE

Autism is a relatively common neurodivergent condition, and we have a multi-generational history of autism in our family. With their permission, I've drawn on their experiences and those of their autistic friends in this book.

It's great to see how many autistic individuals have flourished once they have received the right support. Still, it is important to continue highlighting how schools can adapt their practices to ensure they remain inclusive.

ABOUT THE AUTHOR

Katharine lives in London with her family, including a rescue cat called Billy. She has a degree in Modern Languages and has loved reading and writing since childhood. Katharine was adopted, and her family history and heritage stretches from Iran to Spain to Serbia, as well as Yorkshire and Norfolk.

She works as both a journalist and author and loves both jobs. Most of all, she loves spending time with her family and friends and is happiest when swimming, roving outdoors, or messing about in boats.